# Vascular Plant Inventory of Selected Alpine Areas in Yellowstone National Park

Natural Resource Technical Report NPS/GRYN/NRTR—2012/651

Author

Jennifer Whipple
National Park Service
Yellowstone National Park
P.O. Box 168
Yellowstone, WY 82190


Editor

Nina Chambers
Northern Rockies Conservation Cooperative
P.O. Box 2705
Jackson, WY 83001

December 2012

U.S. Department of the Interior
National Park Service
Natural Resource Stewardship and Science
Fort Collins, Colorado

The National Park Service, Natural Resource Stewardship and Science office in Fort Collins, Colorado, publishes a range of reports that address natural resource topics. These reports are of interest and applicability to a broad audience in the National Park Service and others in natural resource management, including scientists, conservation and environmental constituencies, and the public.

The Natural Resource Technical Report Series is used to disseminate results of scientific studies in the physical, biological, and social sciences for both the advancement of science and the achievement of the National Park Service mission. The series provides contributors with a forum for displaying comprehensive data that are often deleted from journals because of page limitations.

All manuscripts in the series receive the appropriate level of peer review to ensure that the information is scientifically credible, technically accurate, appropriately written for the intended audience, and designed and published in a professional manner.

This report received formal peer review by subject-matter experts who were not directly involved in the collection, analysis, or reporting of the data, and whose background and expertise put them on par technically and scientifically with the authors of the information.

Views, statements, findings, conclusions, recommendations, and data in this report do not necessarily reflect views and policies of the National Park Service, U.S. Department of the Interior. Mention of trade names or commercial products does not constitute endorsement or recommendation for use by the U.S. Government.

This report is available from the Greater Yellowstone Network website (http://science.nature.nps.gov/im/units/gryn/), the Natural Resource Publications Management website (http://www.nature.nps.gov/publications/nrpm/), and the Integration of Natural Resource Management Applications website (https://irma.nps.gov/).

Please cite this publication as:

Whipple, J. 2012. Vascular plant inventory of selected alpine areas in Yellowstone National Park. Natural Resource Technical Report NPS/GRYN/NRTR—2012/651. National Park Service, Fort Collins, Colorado.

NPS 101/118316, December 2012

# Contents

# Figures

# Abstract

High-elevation areas in the Gallatin Mountains and on Cutoff Mountain were investigated (2003-2005) for previously unreported park flora species. Ten new taxa were located: *Anemone tetonensis*; *Antennaria monocephala*; *Claytonia megarhiza*; *Draba crassa*; *Draba globosa*; *Erigeron radicatus*; *Minuartia austromontana*; *Oxytropis deflexa* var. *foliolosa*; *Parnassia kotzebuei*; and *Ranunculus pygmaeus*. The exact determination of two *Draba* specimens, one collected at Cutoff Mountain and another at Quadrant Mountain, is still ongoing with some of the *Draba* specimens sent to the Missouri Botanical Garden to be annotated by Dr. Ihsan Al-Shehbaz. Additionally, *Achnatherum pinetorum* was confirmed to occur in the southern Gallatin Range.

# Acknowledgments

This project was partially funded through the NPS Greater Yellowstone Network Inventory Program. The author would like to thank the NPS inventory steering committee, Rick Lasko, Mason Reid, Ann Rodman, and Kathy Tonnessen for their help conducting the inventory workshop that identified the need for an alpine plant inventory in Yellowstone National Park. The author would also like to thank Cathie Jean and Lane Cameron from the Greater Yellowstone Network for their help on planning the vascular plant inventory. Gallatin National Forest rangers were immensely helpful with the corral operation and fire cache, especially Wally Wines, Dave Elwood, Monty Simenson, Brian Helms, Bonnie Gafney, and Wendy Hafer. The field crews that scrambled here and there included Heidi Anderson, Ken Aho, Vicki Pecha, Elizabeth Crowe, Cheryl Jaworowski, and John David Sacklin. Finally, Mary Hektner was a tower of strength in shepherding the logistics through the years.

# Introduction

One of the goals of the Inventory and Monitoring program of the National Park Service is to have at least a ninety-percent knowledge of the vascular plants of each park unit. The knowledge of the vascular plant flora of Yellowstone National Park is extensive with collections dating back to 1870, but most of the collecting has been focused on areas easily approached from the road system. Botanical surveys during the latter part of the nineteenth century and the early twentieth century were opportunistic, sporadic, and incomplete. An analysis of collecting patterns suggested that in general the areas most under-collected were those approaching treeline or in the alpine zone.

Documentation of the high-elevation flora of the park is made more pressing within the context of global climate change. Species that are currently in restricted habitats associated with remnant ice fields and alpine areas may in the future encounter climatic conditions that could lead to a local extirpation—on a mountain, within a mountain range, or within the entire park. Documentation of the current flora is necessary as a baseline for future knowledge about floristic changes triggered by changing climate and other factors (such as mountain goats, for example).

Due to the road that had been built to the summit, Mount Washburn has been collected extensively through the years, with specimens scattered throughout herbaria in North America. Accessible areas in the Absaroka Range near the road system, such as Republic Pass and Sylvan Pass, have been investigated, but the southern Absarokas, especially in the Thorofare area, have received less attention. Other under-collected areas included the Two Ocean Plateau area and, especially, the Gallatin Range.

Throughout the Absaroka Range and the Two Ocean Plateau, rock types are predominantly Absaroka volcanics. In the Gallatin Range, however, rock types are more variable, including the presence of sedimentary rocks such as limestone, which suggests a greater likelihood for undocumented taxa. Alpine limestone areas in other mountains of the Greater Yellowstone Area have been found to have unique endemics and arctic/alpine plants that are significantly disjunct from the main portion of their ranges. Access in recent years into the Gallatins had been extremely limited due to restrictions implemented for grizzly bear management purposes and human safety over the central part of the range. These restrictions have effectively curtailed botanical exploration and collecting. The presence of areas of limestone in the Gallatin Range near and above treeline elevated the likelihood that undocumented taxa might be present; therefore, this range was targeted in this study for more extensive survey, especially above 9,000 feet in elevation (Figure 1).

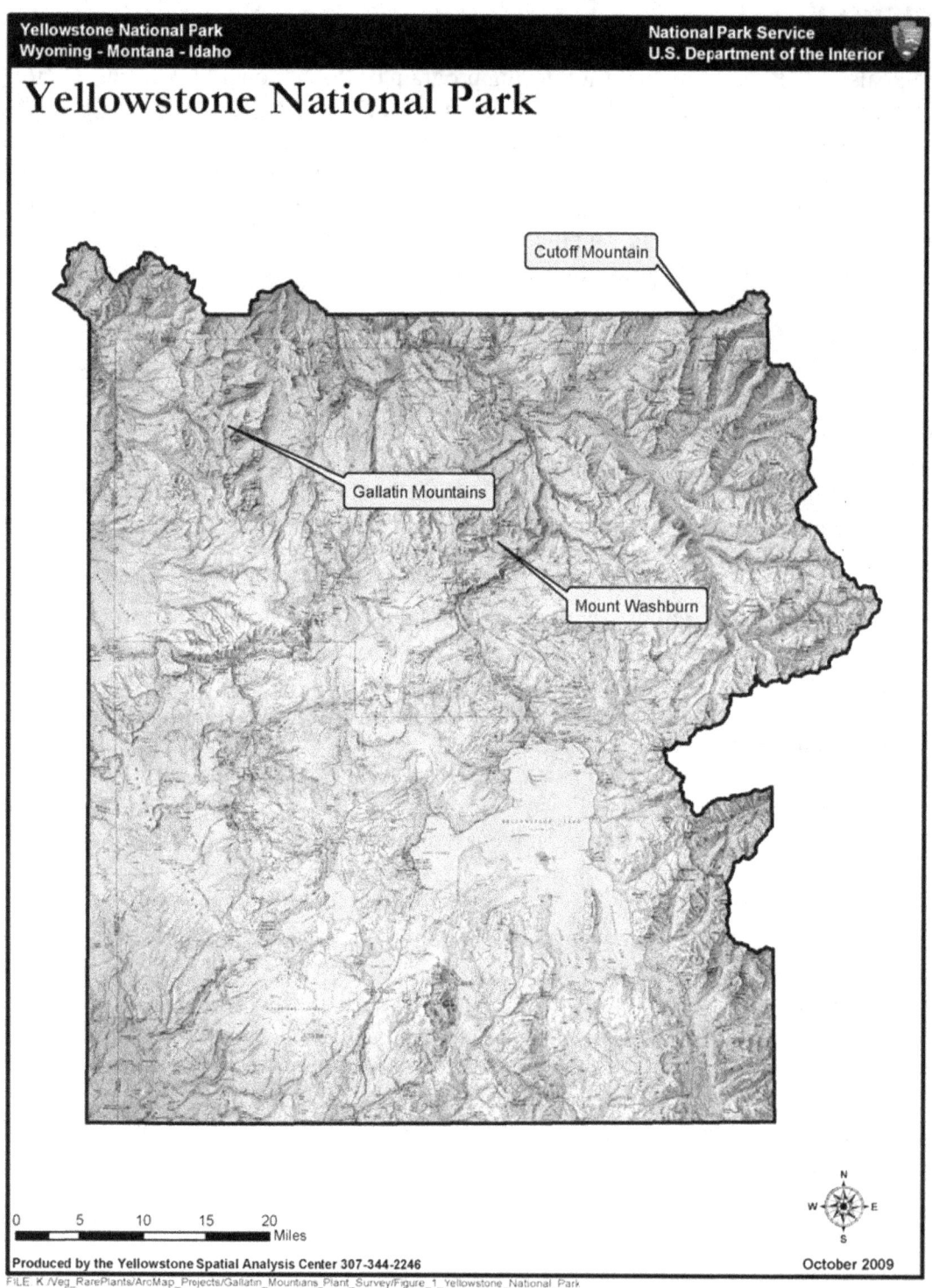

**Figure 1.** Map of Yellowstone National Park showing the general location of the Gallatin Mountain range and Cutoff Mountain study areas. Mount Washburn, an alpine area widely studied due to having a road built to the summit, is shown for reference only.

# Methods

Prior to beginning fieldwork, an extensive analysis of both topographic and geologic maps had suggested possible areas to target survey efforts. An opportunistic helicopter overflight prior to beginning fieldwork allowed a chance to see the proposed study area from the air, providing additional information about accessibility and limestone exposures. The limestone in the vicinity of Fawn Pass (Bannock Peak, Quadrant Mountain) and in the southern portion of the Gallatin Range around Trilobite Ridge was determined to be the highest priority for botanical survey.

Fieldwork in the summer of 2003 included two separate trips into the Gallatin Range. The first trip from July 22 to 29 was based at the Fawn Pass Cabin with supplies brought in by stock. The working crew of six included a packer (Monty Simenson, Dave Elwood) to manage the three horses that remained at the cabin as riding stock, and five botanists (Heidi Anderson, Mary Hektner, Ken Aho, Vicki Pecha, and Jennifer Whipple). Transportation to various field sites utilized horses and foot travel. Some time was lost due to horse complications and inclement weather conditions such as lightning storms. Areas investigated included: Fawn Pass and the ridgeline south of the pass running to the southeast; the northwest ridgeline to the summit of Bannock Peak; the ridge from Fawn Pass to Snowshoe Pass and onto the lower slopes of Gray Peak; the summit of Quadrant Mountain; and the base of the cirque on the north side of Bannock Peak (Figure 3).

The second horse pack trip from August 4 to 7 was based from the Sportsman Lake Cabin to investigate the ridgeline from Electric Pass to Joseph Peak (Figure 4). Personnel included Monty Simenson, packer; Bonnie Gafney, ranger; and Jennifer Whipple, botanist. There was only one day of access to the ridgelines due to horse complications (they left...) and a wildland fire nearby (smokejumpers arrived...). Separately, on August 8 Heidi Anderson climbed Electric Peak looking for additional taxa of interest. The calcareous summit of Antler Peak is inaccessible by either foot or horse, so the decision was made to use a helicopter to access the summit area. Botanists Heidi Anderson and Jennifer Whipple were airlifted on July 10, 2004 for a quick two-hour survey of the summit area, specifically to investigate the possible presence of a rare *Oxytropis* that could have been collected there on July 26, 2001 (Figure 4).

The Trilobite area was targeted for the main field work in 2004, with a base camp established from July 13 to 17 near the trail to Trilobite Lake against the edge of the mountain. The seven field crew members (Heidi Anderson, John David Sacklin, Mary Hektner, Vicki Pecha, Elizabeth Crowe, and Jennifer Whipple) included a geologist (Cheryl Jaworowski) to help the field crew focus on areas that would be most likely to harbor new species to the Yellowstone flora. Pack stock were used to establish the field camp, pack in plant presses, food, and other essentials, but all investigations were done on foot. Sites investigated included: the slope up Trilobite Ridge; Trilobite Lake and the lower slopes of Dome Mountain; and the east slopes of Trilobite Ridge and vicinity of the campsite (Figure 5).

**Figure 2**. Mary Hektner and Heidi Anderson examining plant; above Faw i Pass.

The last horse pack trip was from July 20 to 24, 2005 and again based at the Fawn Pass Patrol Cabin to continue to survey Quadrant Mountain, the west slopes of Gray Peak, and additional investig itions of the Bannock cirque. Field personnel w ere Dave El vood, packer and Jennifer Whipple, botanist (Figure 6).

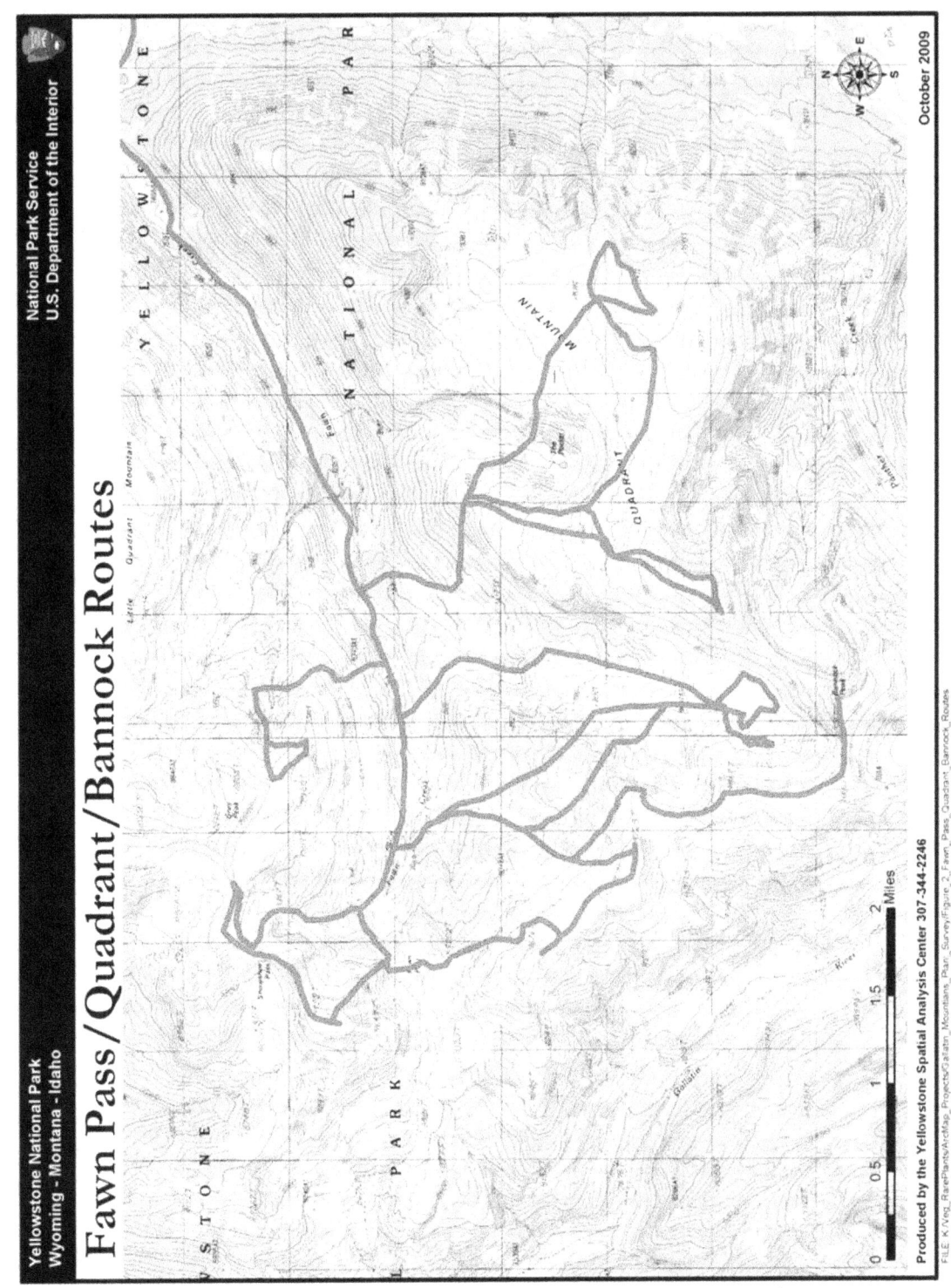

**Figure 3.** Alpine plant survey routes for the Fawn Pass, Quadrant Mountain, and Bannock Peak are is in Yellowstone National Park.

5

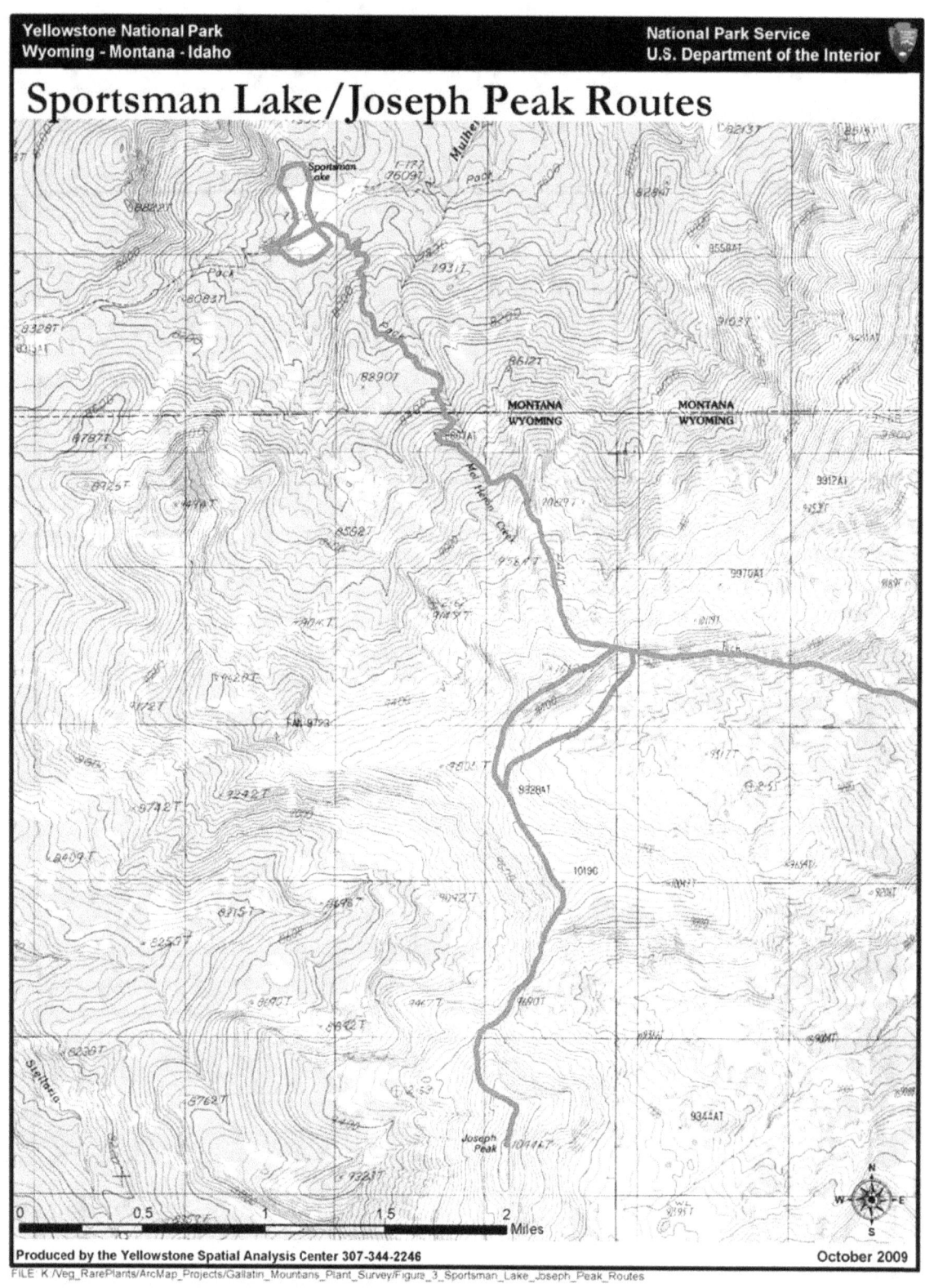

**Figure 4.** Alpine plant survey routes for Sportsman Lake and Joseph Peak in Yellowstone National Park.

6

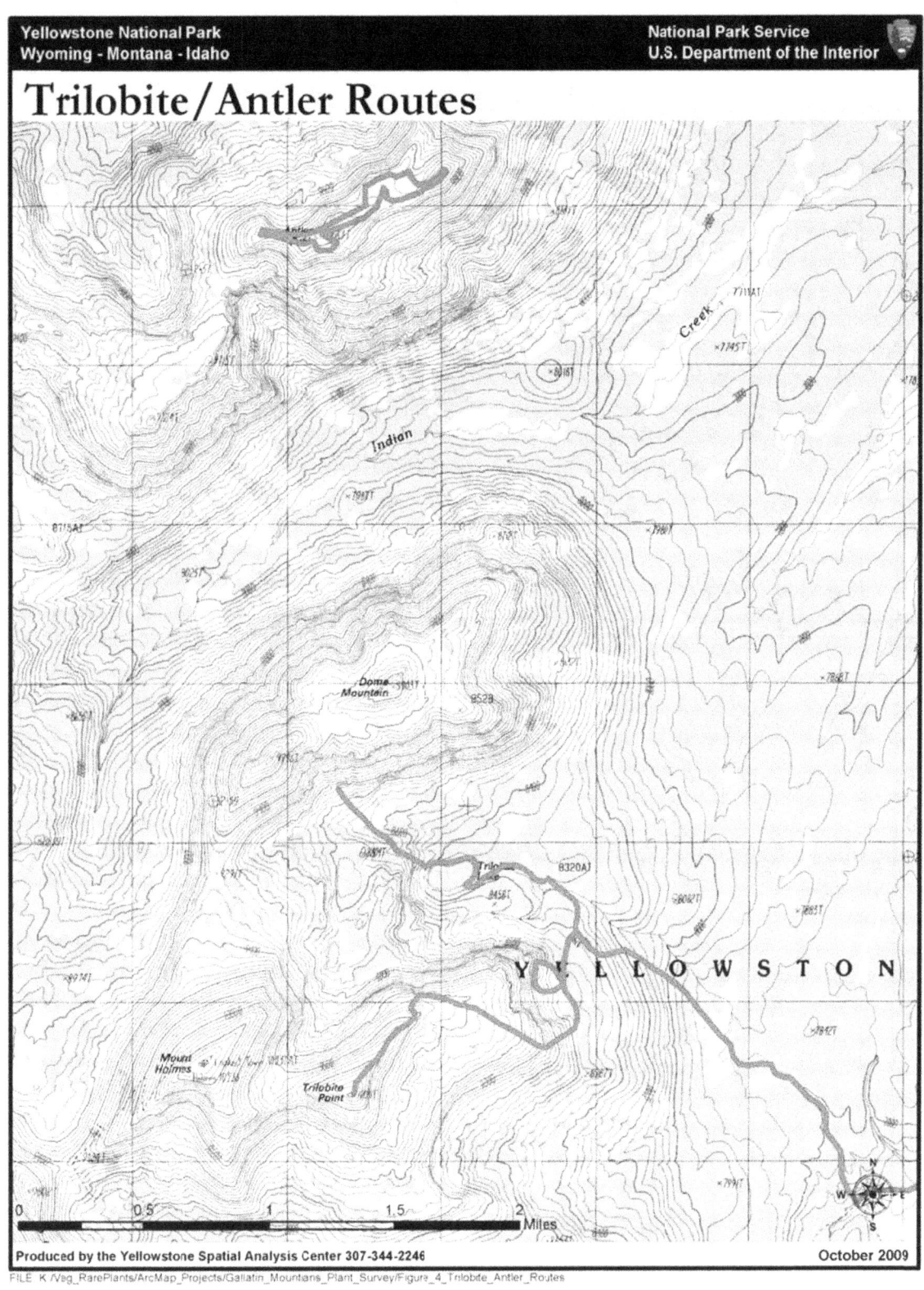

**Figure 5.** Alpine plant survey routes for Trilobite Point and A ıtler Peak in Yellowstone National Park.

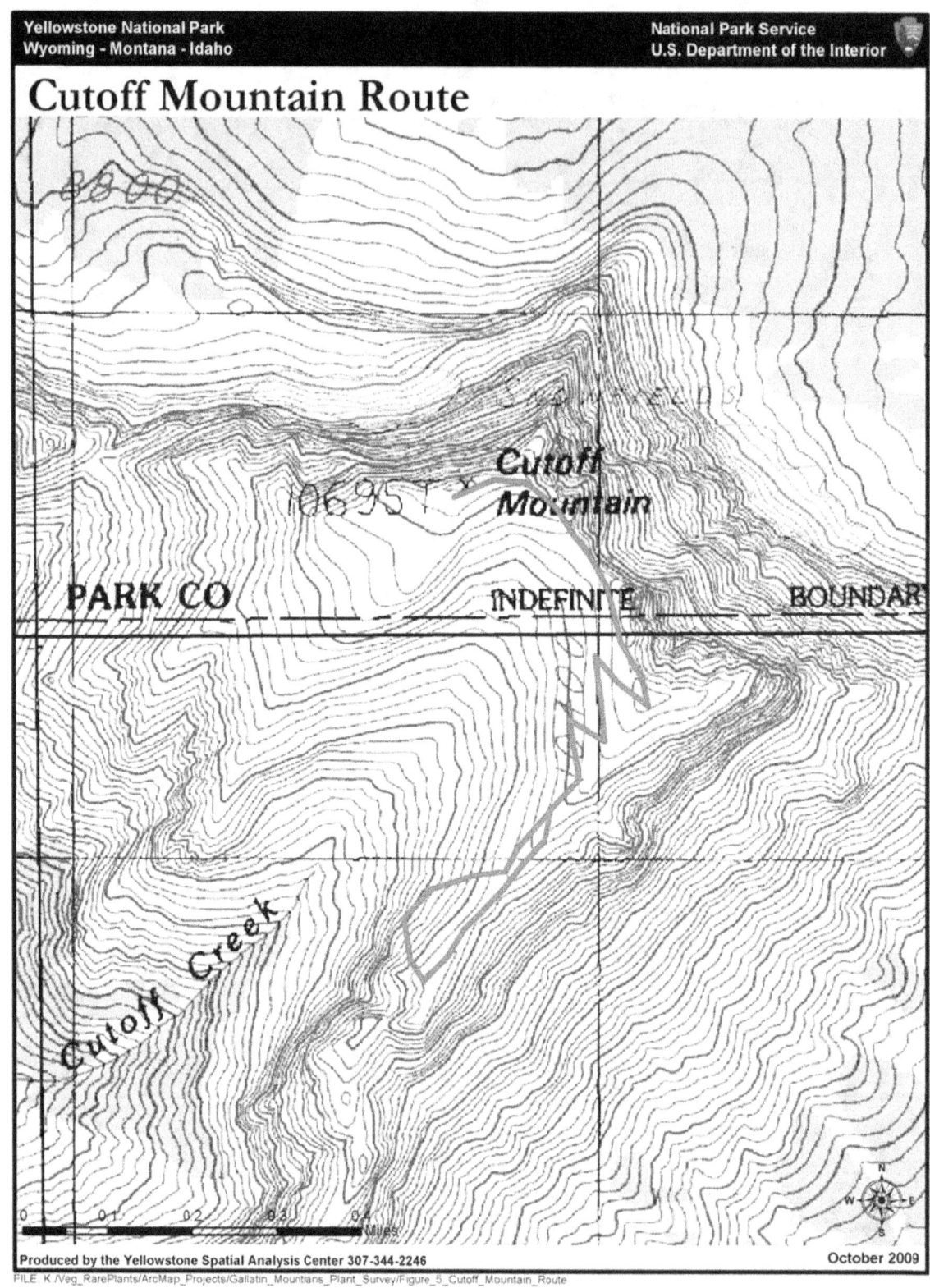

**Figure 6.** Alpine plant survey routes at Cutoff Mountain in Yellowstone National Park.

Ken Aho, who was studying vegetation near treeline in relation to mountain goats in the northeast portion of the park, had located possible new reports for Yellowstone on the summit area of Cutoff Mountain, which is a peak in the Absaroka Range along the north boundary of the park that is largely inaccessible. Ken Aho and Jennifer Whipple were flown by helicopter to near the summit on July 17, 2003 in order to determine if any of these species were actually in Yellowstone Park since the boundary with the Gallatin National Forest runs close to the summit of the mountain. On July 14, 2005, Heidi Anderson and Jennifer Whipple were again flown by helicopter to the summit region to continue investigations, since there were still two species present on the summit that had not been located in the park (Figure 6).

# Results

The fieldwork during the summers of 2003, 2004, and 2005 resulted in 547 collections (460 from the Gallatin Range and 87 from Cutoff Mountain). Most of these specimens were easily identified, but several groups, especially *Draba* and *Erigeron*, needed additional work at the Booth Herbarium at Montana State University (MONT), and the Rocky Mountain Herbarium at the University of Wyoming (RM). The determination of some of the difficult specimens is still ongoing, with some of the *Draba* material sent to the Missouri Botanical Garden to be annotated by Dr. Ihsan Al-Shehbaz.

Documentation of several non-native species present in the Gallatin Mountains was initiated by specimen collection. The first report of *Ranunculus acris* (tall buttercup) in the Gallatin Range was documented at the stock site (WD2) near Sportsman Lake. This species is considered noxious by Montana and is spreading in meadows, especially in the backcountry, which suggests horses are a primary dispersal mechanism. This infestation numbered just two plants which were eradicated. Due to the presence of mature seeds and the fact that there were two plants, this location needs to be monitored in the future to prevent establishment of a nasty infestation.

Twelve new taxa were documented to occur in the park: *Anemone tetonensis*; *Antennaria monocephala*; *Claytonia megarhiza*; *Draba crassa*; *Draba globosa*; *Draba* sp. (Cutoff Mountain), *Draba* sp. (Quadrant Mountain), *Erigeron radicatus*; *Minuartia austromontana*; *Oxytropis deflexa* var. *foliolosa*; *Parnassia kotzebuei*; and *Ranunculus pygmaeus*. Of these, seven were located in the Gallatin Range and the other five were located on Cutoff Mountain. Each of these are discussed below.

*Anemone tetonensis* **Porter ex Britton (Teton anemone)** [*Anemone multifida* Poir. var. *tetonensis* (Porter ex Britton) C. L. Hitchc.]

Teton anemone was first located on the ridge south of Fawn Pass and later located both in the cirque on the north side of Bannock Peak and in talus on Trilobite Peak. This taxon is distributed at high elevations from central Idaho and southern Montana, south to Utah, with outlier populations in the Blue Mountains of northeastern Oregon and in the Charleston Mountains of Nevada (Hitchcock and Cronquist 1964, Flora of North America 1997). Previously unreported for Yellowstone National Park, the appearance of this anemone on calcareous substrates was not unexpected due to its presence in the Teton Mountains south of the park, in the Absaroka Range east of the park, and in the Beartooth Mountains. Coincidentally, this taxon was also found on calcareous substrate later during the summer of 2003 on the Buffalo Plateau at approximately 9,200 feet elevation along the northern boundary of the park.

Figure 7. *Anemone tetonensis* in Bannock Mountain cirque.

11

*Antenn ria monocephala* DC. ssp. *angustata* (Green) Hultén (Si gle-head pussytoes)

Single-h ad pussyto s was located by Ken Aho on top of Cutoff Mountain on the north face just outside f the park boundary on the Gallatin National F rest. The search in 2003 failed to locate any plants within th  park, but a small population was located on the north face of the lower summit f Cutoff M untain in 2005 in an alpine turf co nmunity. T is taxon is primarily arctic in distribut on, occurri g from the Russian Far East (Chuk tka Penins la) across boreal North American to Greenl nd, and down the Rocky Mountain  to Wyoming. Single-head pussytoes is a species f concern i  Wyoming (G4G5/S2) with sites k own from  ost of the high-elevation ranges i  the northw st part of the state. The population in the park was on the more shaded portions of the north and west-facing slopes of the lower ridgecrest  ear the summit of Cutoff Mountai n. Time constraints due to helicopter pick-up restricted the  urvey of the surrounding area, but only the on  area was discovered with two site : one site a proximately 100 meters by 25 mete s, and the o her much smaller, about 10 square meters.

**Figure 8.** *Antennaria  nonocephala* on Cutoff Peak.

*Claytonia megarhiza* (A.Gray) Parry ex S.Watson (Fell-field claytonia)

Fell-field claytonia was located on Cutoff Mountain by Ken Aho and confirmed during the 2003 helicopter trip to be actually in the park on fell-field slopes and rocky talus. The population was small and scattered on the south to west-facing slope of the summit region. This species had previously been collected near the south boundary of the park but most of the trail on Big Game Ridge is outside of the park boundary in the Teton Wilderness, so the presence of this species in the park had remained undetermined. Additional populations of fell-field claytonia are to be expected at high locations in the Absaroka Range, and possibly along the south boundary in the vicinity of Mount Hancock. The center of distribution for this species is in the mountain ranges of the western United States continuing up the Rockies into Canada and the arctic (Flora of North America 2003).

**Figure 9.** *Claytonia megarhiza* on Cutoff Mountain.

***Draba crassa* Rydb. (Thick-leaved draba)**

Thick-leaved draba is a regional endemic known from generally above treeline in the Rocky Mountains from southern Montana to Colorado, and in the Uinta Mountains of Utah. Ken Aho located this species on Cutoff Mountain, but was uncertain as to whether it was within the park. Careful examination of the talus slope and fell field at the park boundary located just a few plants within the approximate boundary of the park. This is the only known location in the park, and most of the population is actually in the Gallatin National Forest. Thick-leaved draba is a Montana plant species of concern (G3G4/S2S3) and is known from Beaverhead, Deer Lodge, Granite, Madison, and Park counties, while in Wyoming the species is know from Absaroka, Wind River, Teton, and Gros Ventre ranges (WYNDD 1999).

**Figure 1 ).** *Draba crassa* on Cutoff Mountain.

*Draba globosa* Payson (**Beaver-tip draba**)

Beaver-tip draba is a regional endemic of southwestern Montana ( adison and Centennial ranges), Wyoming, entral Colorado, south-central Idaho, and northwestern Utah. Frequently found o high elevation calcareous substrates, this speci s was one of the suspected possible target species for the survey in the Gallatin Range. Sites were located on both Antler Peak and Quadrant Mountain on calcareous substrates. The Quad ant Mountain site was in a rocky creviced area near the summit of the mountain on a gradual north-facing slope. Two different location were discovered on Antler Peak: one near the summit by a melting south-facing snow bank, th other growing on the northeast-facing slope of the summit in a tundra/meadow. In all three locations, the umber of plants was small: about 2 5 plants nea the pond on Quadrant Mountain; at least 2 plants near the snow bank on Antler Peak where more habitat may have been ex osed later i the season; and about 25 plants on the northw st slope near the summit, which h d recently elted off. Both Antler Peak and Q adrant Mountain may harbor additional sites. Beaver-tip dra a is on the Wyoming species of co cern list (G3/S2S3) and on the Montana species f concern list (G3/S2S3) from Beaverhead and Madison counties, and on the Idaho list (G3/S2).

**Figure 1 I.** *Draba globosa* on Antler Peak.

***Draba* s ). (Cutoff  Iountain)**

This tax )n is currently being reviewed by the authority  )n *Draba,* Dr. Ihsan Al-Shehbaz at the Missour  Botanic G  rden. This taxon is clearly a new report for the  )ark but the correct identific ition is pen ling. The material from Cutoff Mountain lacks  iny appreciable hairs on the leaves.  'he inconspicuous plants were located on a moi  t turf com   unity in shaded nooks and crannies among the  'ocks, with only about 20 plants loc ited, so ver ' little material was collected, which may contribute to uncertainties about the identifi  ation of this population.

**Figure 1** !. *Draba* sp.  )n Cutoff Mountain.

## *Draba* sp. (Quadrant Mountain)

This plant is an inconspicuous white-flowered mustard that was located on Quadrant Mountain scattered among talus on the north face of the red mound on the eastern side of the flat summit area. The few plants (less than 25) were tucked among boulders (as can be seen in figure 13) in moist soil in an area dominated by *Mertensia ciliata*. Also present were *Polemonium viscosum*, *Erigeron compositus*, *Draba incerta*, and *Saxifraga rivularis*. This taxon does not appear to be represented in the Flora of North American (Flora of North America 2010) key to Draba and could represent a previously undescribed entity. Dr. Ihsan Al-Shehbaz who is a noted expert in the *Brassicaceae*, is examing the material.

Figure 13. Red mound on top of Quadrant Mountain, habitat of *Draba* sp.

Figure 14. *Draba* sp. on Quadrant Mountain.

17

*Erigeron radicatus* Hook. (**Taproot fleabane**)

Taproot fleabane was located on Antler Peak and Trilobite Point in the Gallatin Range during survey of those areas. The populations were extremely small and scattered among talus and rock outcrops on both peaks, numbering just a few individuals in total, limiting the collections to just single individuals. In-depth survey would be time consuming and difficult since the plants are often hard to locate in the rocks, and the focus of this study was to cover as much ground as possible. Taproot fleabane is found from Alberta and Saskatchewan in Canada, down the Rocky Mountains into Wyoming and Utah, and east to the Dakotas and Nebraska. This species is usually found on calcareous substrates such as limestone, which is the case in the Gallatin Range. Within Wyoming, *Erigeron radicatus* is known from northwest Wyoming in the Absaroka, northwest Wind River, Gros Ventre, and Wyoming ranges (WYNDD 1996). Distinguishing this species from *E. ochroleucus* is difficult, and earlier collections from the Gallatin Range that were identified as *E. ochroleucus* may in fact be *E. radicatus*. All of the high-elevation specimens of these two taxa need to be carefully examined in the future. *Erigeron* is a notorious genus taxonomically. Unfortunately, no photos were taken since the significance of the specimens was not realized until examined in the herbarium later.

**Figure 15.** Antler Peak summit area, habitat *of Erigeron radicatus, Oxytropis deflexa* var. *foliolosa, Minuartia austromontana*, and *Draba globosa*.

18

## *Minuartia austrom ntana* S. J. Wolf & Packer (Rocky Mountain sandwort)

Rocky Iountain sa dwort is usually found on dry rock calcareous slopes and fell-fields in
alpine areas (Flora of North America 2005), which is ex actly where it was located in the Gallatin
Range. his species was discovered at several locations including Antler Peak, Bannock Peak,
and Trilobite Point. There were healthy numbers of plants at these sites, especially on the slopes
of Trilo ite Point w ere it occurs in a rocky pavement. Rocky Mountain sandwort occurs from
British 'olumbia an d Alberta in Canada, south to Oregon, and east o Wyoming and Utah. The
Wyoming sites are primarily concentrated in northwestern Wyomin g around Yellowstone
National Park, so th presence of this species in the par was not su prising.

**Figure 1 ).** *Minuartia austromontana* on Trilobite Point.

### *Oxytropis deflexa* var. *foliolosa* (Hook.) Barneby (Nodding alpine locoweed)

Nodding alpine locoweed is the high-elevation variety of the more commonly encountered *Oxytropis deflexa* var. *deflexa*, which is scattered around the park in meadows and wetland edges. Nodding alpine locoweed was first encountered in fruit on Antler Peak when the summit was visited by helicopter on July 26, 2001. The specimen was just a fragment and the determination was somewhat problematic. The survey on the summit of Antler Peak in July 2004 confirmed the presence of nodding alpine locoweed. Later that summer, a population on Trilobite Point was also discovered. At both sites, the number of individuals is small, with the plants associated with *Dryas octopetala* in a dense tundra-like mat. This taxon is considered to be a glacial relict in tundra and alpine meadow in the southern portion of its range, occurring from Nevada to Colorado north into the arctic with cognate or possibly identical forms in east Asia. This species is currently tracked by Montana (G5 3T5/S2S3) with one known occurrence in the Madison Range, and formerly tracked by the Wyoming Natural Diversity Database where it has been found to be more common, especially on high elevation calcareous substrates in the western portion of the state.

**Figure 1 7.** *Oxytropis deflexa* var. *foliolosa* on Trilobite Ridge.

*Parnassia kotzebuei* **Cham. ex Spreng (Kotzebue's grass-of-parnassus)**

Kotzebue's grass-of parnassus was located on steep north-facing slopes above the cirque on the north face of Bannock Peak. Ken Aho used his rock-climbing skills to investigate some of these slopes and found a patch of Kotzebue's grass-of-parnassus and brought it back up to the ridgecrest. The steepness of the terrain prevented exploration of the site by the rest of the field crew, so there are no estimates of population size or photographs of this species. Kotzebue's grass-of-parnassus i circumpolar occurring across the Canadian arctic and Alaska, extending into the western United States including the Ruby Mountains in Nevada, Colorado, Washington Idaho, Montana, and Wyoming were it is primarily known in the mountain ranges in the western portion of the state. This species was one of the target species of the investigation in the Gallatin Range, since it was documented in the Greater Yellowstone Area.

Figure 13. Bannock Peak cirque, habitat of *Parnassia kotzebuei.*

21

*Ranunculus pygmaeus* Wahlenb. (Pygmy buttercup)

Pygmy buttercup is an arctic species that occurs from Alaska to Greenland and Spitsbergen with relict populations in locations such as the Alps, stretching south along the mountains of the western cordilleran into the Rockies of Montana, Wyoming, and south to Colorado. Pygmy buttercup was first located by Ken Aho on the north face of Cutoff Mountain in the Gallatin National Forest. The first search of the Yellowstone side of the summit failed to locate any buttercup, but a later search of the north slope of the lower southern summit area successfully located this species. The first site located was on the north side of a large boulder, with additional plants located in the shady areas around nearby boulders. The plants numbered at least 200 individuals in an area approximately 30 meters by 10 meters. Plants were scattered within that area in the alpine turf community. Being restricted to very high elevations, this species is of conservation concern in parts of the Rocky Mountains. There is only one known population in Idaho where it is considered a G5/S1, while it is more common in Wyoming and Montana where it is not currently tracked by the heritage programs.

**Figure 10.** *Ranunculus pygmaeus* on Cutoff Mountain.

22

## Additional Species Collected

Several other notable collections were made, including the confirmation of *Achnatherum pinetorum* (M. E. Jones) Barkworth, at two locations in the Gallatin Range. A fragment of material had come into the herbarium years previously from a wildlife study conducted in the Gallatin's that appeared to be this species, but there was no information about exact location where the sample fragment was collected. Healthy sites were found on rocky substrates, especially in the Trilobite region.

*Draba paysonii* J.F. Macbr. var. *paysonii,* is a species of concern in Wyoming (G5T3/S2), was located at two locations: near Fawn Pass, and on the summit of Antler Peak. In both cases there were very few plants growing in the rocky talus, but the individual plants were relatively large, allowing collections to document the presence of this taxon.

A vascular plant species list was generated of all of the species collected in the Gallatin Range during this study (Appendix A). Additionally, a vascular plant species list of all taxa known to occur at or above 9,000 feet in elevation in Yellowstone National Park was initiated (Appendix B), though this list is known to be incomplete at this time. (The lists presented in Appendices A and B are provisional and subject to change.)

# Discussion

Botanical exploration of the park is still ongoing. The flora of Yellowstone is clearly well known above the ninety percent level, but there are still new species to be located. The rarest species in the park are the plants that are extremely limited in distribution. The corollary is that these taxa are difficult to locate since they could be scattered almost anywhere, but in recent years most new additions to the park flora have occurred on the barren slopes near and in the Gardiner Basin at the lowest elevations in the park; in wetlands, especially in the Bechler region; and at the highest elevations near and above treeline.

Due to the nearby presence of the Beartooth Mountains and the higher summits of the Absaroka Range east of the park boundary, there is a reservoir of alpine species known to occur on these peaks that have not been located in the park at this time. Some of these alpine species are likely to be present. Among those areas to explore more extensively include additional locations in the Gallatin Range, especially the higher elevation limestone/calcareous outcrops such as Dome Mountain; and the Absaroka Range, especially in the Thorofare region, since remoteness has limited botanical exploration there in the past. Other possible areas of interest are Mount Hancock on the northern edge of Big Game Ridge, the Two Ocean Plateau, and the peaks in the northeast corner of the park, such as Amphitheater Mountain where Ken Aho has located an additional species for the park flora, *Phyllodoce glandulifera*. As demonstrated by this study, areas at treeline and higher elevations into the true alpine zone still harbor numerous species that are extremely limited in distribution. These plants are most likely on north-facing slopes and cliffs and other locations difficult to explore. Whenever possible, high peaks should be carefully examined for additional species that may be lurking in crevices, rock piles, and, of course, in plain view.

# References

Flora of North America Editorial Committee. 1997. Flora of North America North of Mexico, Volume 3: Magnoliophyta: Magnoliidae and Hamamelidae. Oxford University Press, New York, New York.

Flora of North America Editorial Committee. 2003. Flora of North America North of Mexico, Volume 4: Magnoliophyta: Carylphyllidae, Part 1. Oxford University Press, New York, New York.

Flora of North America Editorial Committee. 2005. Flora of North America North of Mexico, Volume 5: Magnoliophyta: Caryophyllidae, Part 2. Oxford University Press, New York, New York.

Flora of North America Editorial Committee. 2010. Flora of North America North of Mexico, Volume 7: Magnoliophyta, Salicaceae to Brassicaceae. Oxford University Press, New York, New York.

Hitchcock, C. L. and A. Cronquist. 1964. Part 2: Salicaceae to Saxifragaceae. In Hitchcock, C.L., A. Cronquist, M. Ownbey, and J.W. Thompson. 1955-1969. Vascular Plants of the Pacific Northwest, 5 vols. University of Washington Press, Seattle. 597 pp..

Wyoming Natural Diversity Database. 1999. State Species Abstract. *Draba crassa,* Walter Fertig 99-12-08. Online. (http://www.uwyo.edu/wynddsupport/docs/Reports/SpeciesAbstracts/Draba_crassa.pdf). Accessed 22 October 2009.

Wyoming Natural Diversity Database. 1996. State Species Abstract. *Erigeron radicatus* (Taprooted Fleabane), Stephanie Mills and Walter Fertig 1996. Online. (http://www.uwyo.edu/wynddsupport/docs/Reports/SpeciesAbstracts/Erigeron_radicatus.pdf) Accessed 22 October 2009.

# Appendix A: List of Specimens Collected During the 2003, 2004, and 2005 Field Seasons on the Gallatin Range in Yellowstone National Park

*Note: This list is provisional and subject to change.*

A = Antler Peak
B = Bannock Peak
F = Fawn Pass and vicinity
G = Gray Peak
J = Joseph Peak
Q = Quadrant Mountain
S = Sportsman Lake
T = Trilobite Point and vicinity

## ADIANTACEAE
*Pellaea breweri* D. C. Eaton: Q, T

## ASPLENIACEAE
*Cystopteris fragilis* (L.) Bernh.: B

## APIACEAE
*Angelica arguta* Nutt.: S
*Angelica roseana* Henderson: F
*Bupleuron americanum* Coult. & Rose: A, F, J, Q
*Lomatium cous* (Wats.) Coult. & Rose: J
*Lomatium dissetum* (Nutt.) Math. & Const.var. *multifidum* (Nutt.) Math. & Const.: T
*Lomatium triternatum* (Pursh) Coult. & Rose var. *platycarpum* (Torrey) Boivin: F, T

## ASTERACEAE
*Achillea milleforium* L. var. *lanulosa* (Nutt.) Piper: F
*Agoseris glauca* (Pursh) Raf. var. *dasycephala* (T. & G.) Jeps.: B
*Agoseris glauca* (Pursh) Raf. var. *laciniata* (Eaton) Smiley: B
*Agoseris lackschewitzii* Henderson & Moseley: T
*Antennaria corymbosa* E. Nels.: Q
*Antennaria media* Greene: B, Q
*Antennaria microphylla* Rydb.: B
*Antennaria umbrinella* Rydb: B, Q
*Arnica chamissonis* Less var. *foliosa* (Nutt.) Maguire: S
*Arnica longifolia* Eaton: B
*Arnica mollis* Hook.: G
*Arnica rydbergii* Greene: B, F
*Artemisia frigida* Willd.: B
*Artemisia ludoviciana* Nutt.var. *latiloba* Nutt.: F
*Balsamorhiza sagittata* (Pursh) Nutt.: T
*Chaenactis alpina* (Gray) Jones: F, J

*Cirsium eatonii* (Gray) Robins.: B, F
*Ericameria suffruticosa* (Nutt.) Nesom: F
*Erigeron acris* L. var. *kamtschaticus* (DC.) Herder: G
*Erigeron compositus* Pursh var. *discoideus* Gray: B, F
*Erigeron lonchophyllus* Hook.: Q
*Erigeron radicatus* Hook.: A, T
*Erigeron rydbergii* Cronq.: B, J, Q
*Erigeron simplex* Greene: B, Q
*Erigeron ursinus* D. C. Eaton: A, B, F, G
*Eriophyllum lanatum* (Pursh) Forbes var. *integrifolium* (Hook.) Smiley: T
*Hieracium triste* Willd. ex Spreng. var. *gracile (*Hook.) Gray: Q
*Hulsea algida* Gray: J
*Oreostemma alpigenum* (T. & G.) Greene var. *haydenii* (Porter) Nesom: B, F
*Packera dimorphophyla* (Greene) Weber & Löve
        var. *paysonii* (Barkley) Trock & Barkley: Q
*Senecio integerrimus* Nutt. var. *exaltatus* (Nutt.) Cronq.: B, F, T
*Senecio fremontii* T. & J. var. *fremontii*: B, J
*Senecio lugens* Richardson: B, Q
*Solidago multiradiata* Ait. var. *scopulorum* Gray: A, B, F
*Stenotus acaulis* (Nutt.) Nutt.: B, F
*Symphyotrichum foliaceum* (Lindl. ex DC.) Nesom var. *apricum* (Gray) Nesom: B, F
*Taraxacum ceratophorum* (Ledeb.) DC.: B
*Taraxacum laevigatum* (Willd.) DC.: F, B
*Taraxacum officinale* Weber: T
*Taraxacum scopulorum* (Gray) Weber: B, G, J
*Townsendia alpigena* Piper: A, F
*Townsendia parryi* D. C. Eaton: F, Q
*Townsendia spathulata* Nutt.: J

## BORAGINACEAE
*Eritrichium nanum* (Vill.) Schrad. ex Gaudin var. *elongatum* (Rydb.) Cronq.: A, J
*Hackelia micrantha* (Eastw.) Gentry: F, T
*Hackelia patens* (Nutt.) Johnston var. *patens*: T
*Mertensia alpina* (Torrey) G. Don: A, Q
*Mertensia ciliata* (James ex Torrey) G. Don var. ciliata: B, T
*Mertensia viridis* (A. Nels.) A. Nels.: F
*Myosotis alpestris* Schmidt: B

## BRASSICACEAE
*Boechera angustifolium* (Nutt.) Dorn: Q
*Boechera lemmonii* (Wats.) Weber var. *lemmonii*: F
*Boechera lyallii* (Wats.) Dorn: Q
*Boechera nuttallii* (Robins.) Dorn: A, F, Q
*Boechera sparsiflora* (Nutt.) Dorn var. *subvillosa* (Wats.) Dorn: T
*Cardamine oligosperma* Nutt.: J, T
*Descurainia incana* (Bernh. ex Fisch. & Meyer) Dorn var. *incana* : F

*Descurainia incana* (Bernh. ex Fisch. & Meyer) Dorn
var. *macrosperma* (Schulz) Dorn : G
*Draba cana* Rydb. B, G, Q
*Draba crassifolia* Grah.: A, G, Q
*Draba globosa* Payson: A, Q
*Draba incerta* Payson: F, Q, T
*Draba lonchocarpa* Rydb. var. *lonchocarpa*: A, B, T
*Draba oligosperma* Hook.: A, B, F, J, T
*Draba paysonii* Macbr. var. *paysonii:* A, F
*Draba praelta* Greene: T
*Draba porsildii* Mulligan: Q
*Erysimum inconspicuum* (Wats.) MacM.: T
*Physaria didymocarpa* (Hook.) Gray var. *didymocarpa*: A, J
*Physaria integrifolia* (Rollins) Lichvar: J
*Smelowskia calycina* (Steph. ex Willd.) Meyer
var. *americana* (Regel & Herder) Drury & Rollins : A, B, Q

## CARYOPHYLLACEAE

*Cerastium arvense*: A, B, J
*Eremogone congesta* (Nutt.) Ikonnikov var. *congesta*: Q
*Minuartia austromontana* S.J.Wolf & Packer: A, B, T
*Minuartia nuttallii* (Pax) Briq. var. *nuttallii*: F
*Minuartia obtusiloba* (Rydb.) House: A, B, G, Q
*Minuartia rubella* (Wahl.) Hiem: A, B, T
*Sagina saginoides* (L.) Karsten G
*Silena acaulis* (L.) Jacq var. subacaulescens: A, B, Q
*Stellaria crispa* Cham. & Schlecht: S
*Stellaria longipes* Goldie var. longipes: B
*Silene parry* (Wats.) Hitchc. & Maguirei: F
*Stellaria umbellata* Turcz.: G

## CRASSULACEAE

*Sedum lanceolatum* Torrey: B, F
*Sedum integrifolium* (Raf.) A. Nels.: B

## CYPERACEAE

*Carex albonigra* Mack.: G, J
*Carex disperma* Dewey: S
*Carex elynoides* Holm.: A, B, G, Q
*Carex epapillosa* Mack.: G, T
*Carex haydeniana* Olney: B, F, G, Q, T
*Carex illota* Bailey: T
*Carex micropoda* C. A. Meyer: G
*Carex microptera* Mack.: S
*Carex neurophora* Mack.: G, S, T
*Carex paysonis* Clokey: Q

*Carex pelocarpa* Hermann: B, Q
*Carex phaeocephala* Piper: B, F, G, Q
*Carex raynoldsii* Dewey: F, G
*Carex rossii* Boott: T
*Carex rupestris* Allioni: T
*Carex scirpoidea* Michx. var. *pseudoscirpoidea* (Rydb.) Dunlop: A, B
*Carex scopulorum* Holm: T
*Carex subnigricans* Stacey: B
*Carex tahoensis* Smiley: F

## ERICACEAE
*Arctostaphylos uva-ursi* (L.) Spreng: A
*Kalmia microphylla* (Hook.) Heller var. *microphylla*: T

## FABACEAE
*Astragalus alpinus* L.: F, J, T
*Astragalus australis* (L.) Lam. var. *glabriusculus* (Hook.) Isely: F, J, Q, T
*Astragalus kentrophyta* Gray var. *tegetarius* (Wats.) Dorn: A, Q
*Astragalus miser* Dougl. var. *hylophilus* (Rydb.) Barneby: F
*Hedysarum sulphurescens* Rydb.: A, B
*Oxytropis borealis* DC. var. *viscida* (Nutt.) Welsh: A, F
*Oxytropis campestris* (L.) DC. var. *cusickii* (Greenm.) Barneby: A, B, J, Q, T
*Oxytropis deflexa* var. *foliolosa* (Hook.) Barneby: A, T
*Oxytropis sericea* Nutt. var. *speciosa* (T. & G.) Welsh: A, T
*Trifolium haydenii* Porter: A, F
*Trifolium longipes* Nutt. var. *reflexum* A. Nels.: T
*Trifolium parryi* Gray var. *montanense* (Rydb.) Welsh: A, F, G, Q, J

## GROSSULARIACEAE
*Ribes lacustre* (Pers.) Poiret: S
*Ribes montigenum* McClatchie: F

## HYDROPHYLLACEAE
*Phacelia hastata* Dougl. ex Lehm var. *hastata*: F
*Phacelia sericea* (Grah. ex Hook.) Gray var. *sericea*: F, G

## JUNCACEAE
*Juncus drummondii* Meyer: B, G, Q
*Juncus mertensianus* Bong.: G
*Luzula parviflora* (Ehrh.) Desv.: T
*Luzula spicata* (L.) DC.: B, G, Q

## LILIACEAE
*Lloydia serotina* (L.) Salisbury ex Reichenback var. *serotina*: A, B
*Zygadenus elegans* Pursh: A, B

ONAGRACEAE

    *Epilobium ciliatum* Raf. var. *glandulosum* (Lehm.) Dorn: G
    *Epilobium clavatum* Trel.: G
    *Epilobium halleanum* Hausskn.: A, B, G, Q
    *Epilobium saximontanum* Hausskn.: G, T

ORCHIDACEAE

    *Listera cordata* (L.) R. Br.: T
    *Platanthera stricta* Lindl.: T

OROBANCHACEAE

    *Orobanche uniflora* L. var. *occidentalis* (Greene) Taylor & MacBryde: B

PARNASSIACEAE

    *Parnassia fimbriata* Konig: B
    *Parnassia kotzebuei* Cham. ex Spreng.: B

PLANTAGINACEAE

    *Plantago tweedyi* Gray: F, G

POACEAE

    *Achnatherum nelsonii* (Scribn.) Barkw. ssp. *dorei* (Barkw. & Maze) Dorn: T
    *Achnatherum pinetorum* (Jones) Barkw.: T
    *Calamagrostis purpurescens* R. Br.: A
    *Cinna latifolia* (Trevir. ex Goepp.) Griseb.: S
    *Deschampsia cespitosa* (L.) Beauv. var. *cespitosa*: F, Q
    *Elymus spicatus* (Pursh) Gould: F
    *Festuca brachyphylla* Schultes & Schultes var. *coloradensis* (Frederiksen) Dorn: G, J
    *Melica bulbosa* Geyer ex Porter & Coult.: F, T
    *Phleum alpinum* L.: B, Q
    *Poa alpina* L. ssp. *alpina*: A, B, J, Q, T
    *Poa arctica* R. Br. var. *grayana* (Vasey) Dorn: A
    *Poa cusickii* Vasey var. *epilis* (Scribn.) C. L. Hitchc.: B, G, T
    *Poa fendleriana* (Steud.) Vasey ssp. *fendleriana*: T
    *Poa leptocoma* Trin.: S
    *Poa palustris* L.: T
    *Poa pratensis* L.: J, T
    *Poa rupicola* Nash ex Rydb: Q
    *Poa secunda* Presl ssp. *secunda*: A
    *Podagrostis humilis* (Vasey) Björkman: S, T

POLEMONIACEAE

    *Phlox multiflora* A. Nels.: A, B, F
    *Phlox pulvinata* (Wherry) Cronq.: A, B, T
    *Polemonium viscosum* Nutt.: A, B

POLYGONACEAE

*Eriogonum ovalifolium* Nutt. var. *purpureum* (Nutt.) Durand.: A, B
*Eriogonum umbellatum* Torr. var. *dichrocephalum* Gandoger: T
*Oxyria digyna* (L.) Hill: B, G
*Bistorta distortoides* (Pursh) Small: B, F
*Bistorta vivipara* (L.) Delarbre: B

PRIMULACEAE

*Androsace septentrionalis* L. var. *subulifera* Gray: J
*Dodecatheon pulchellum* (Raf.) Merr. var. *pulchellum*: A

RANUNCULACEAE

*Anemone multifida* Poiret: B, F
*Anemone parviflora* Michx.: B
*Anemone tetonensis* Porter ex Britton: F, T
*Aquilegia flavescens* Wats.: F, T
*Ranunculus acris* L. var. *acris*: S
*Ranunculus eschscholtzii* Schlecht. var. *eschscholtzii*: J
*Ranunculus eschscholtzii* Schlecht var. *eximius* (Greene) Benson: F, G, J
*Thalictrum occidentale* Gray: S, T

ROSACEAE

*Dryas octapetala* L. var. *hookeriana* (Juz.) Breit.: A, B, T
*Geum triflorum* Pursh var. *ciliatum* (Pursh) Fassett: B
*Geum rossii* (R. Br.) Ser. var. *turbinatum* (Rydb.) C. L. Hitchc.: J
*Ivesia gordonii* (Hook.) T. & G.: F, J, T
*Potentilla diversifolia* Lehm. var. *diversifolia*: B, F, G, J
*Potentilla diversifolia* Lehm. var. *perdissecta* (Rydb.) Hitchc.: A, B, T
*Potentilla glandulosa* Lindl. var. *pseudorupestris* (Rydb.) Breit.: B, F
*Potentilla gracilis* Dougl. ex Hook. var. *fastigiata* (Nutt.) Watson: T
*Potentilla gracilis* Dougl. var. *pulcherrima* (lehm.) Sheld.: B
*Potentilla ovina* Macoun var. *ovina*: A, Q, T
*Potentilla rubricaulis* Lehm.: B, F, Q

RUBIACEAE

*Galium bifolium* Wats.: B, G

SALICACEAE

*Salix arctica* Pallas var. *petraea* (Anderss.) Bebb: B, Q
*Salix barclayi* Anderss.: S
*Salix drummondiana* Barr. ex Hook. F
*Salix eastwoodiae* Cock. ex Heller: F
*Salix pseudomonticola* Ball: S
*Salix reticulata* L. var.. *nivalis* (Hook.) Anderss. : A, T
*Salix rotundifolia* Trautv. var. *dodgeana* (Rydb.) E. Murray: A
*Salix tweedyi* (Bebb ex Rose) Ball: F, S

## SAXIFRAGACEAE
*Heuchera parvifolia* Nutt. ex T. & G. : T
*Lithophragma glabrum* Nutt. var. *ramulosum* (Suksd.) Boivin: B
*Saxifraga bronchialis* L. var. *austromontana* (Wieg.) Piper ex G. N. Jones: T
*Saxifraga cespitosa* L. var. *minima* Blank.: B, T
*Saxifraga odontoloma* Piper: B
*Saxifraga oppositifolia* L.: A, B
*Saxifraga rivularis* L.: G, Q
*Saxifraga rhomboidea* Greene: A, Q
*Saxifraga subpetala* E. Nels.: B
*Telesonix heucheriiformis* (Rydb.) Rydb.: B

## SELAGINELLACEAE
*Selaginella densa* Rydb. var. *scopulorum* (Maxon) R. M. Tryon: A, J, Q

## SCROPHULARIACEAE
*Besseya wyomingensis* (A. Nels.) Rydb.: F
*Castilleja cristagalli* Rydb.: F, T
*Castilleja pallescens* (Gray) Greenm.: F
*Castilleja pulchella* Rydb.: A, B, J
*Castilleja rhexifolia* Rydb.: B
*Castilleja sulphurea* Rydb.: B, F
*Mimulus suksdorfii* Gray: T
*Pedicularis bracteosa* Benth. var. *paysoniana* (Pennell) Cronq.: T
*Pedicularis contorta* Benth. var. *contorta*: B
*Pedicularis groenlandica* Retz.: B
*Pedicularis parryi* Gray var. *purpurea* C. Parry: B, F, Q
        Hybrid between *P. contorta* and *P. parryi*: B
*Penstemon attenuatus* Dougl. ex Lindl. var. *pseudoprocerus* (Rydb.) Cronq.: B, F, T
*Penstemon deustus* Dougl. ex Lindl.: T
*Penstemon montanus* Greene var. *montanus*: F
*Penstemon procerus* Dougl. ex Grah var. *procerus*: Q
*Veronica americana* Schwein. ex Benth.: B
*Veronica wormskjoldii* R. & S.: Q

## VALERIANACEAE
*Valeriana acutiloba* Rydb. var. *pubicarpa* (Rydb.) Cronq.: F, G, T
*Valeriana occidentalis* Heller: T

## VIOLACEAE
*Viola adunca* Smith: F
*Viola palustri* L.: T
*Viola praemosa* Dougl. ex Lindl. var. *altior* Blank.: F, T

# Appendix B: Alpine and Tree Line Vascular Plant Species List in Yellowstone National Park

The determination of tree line is problematic due to the variation among different peaks, ranges, and the various definitions of tree line and alpine. This list documents vascular plants known to occur above 9,000 feet in elevation in the park, recognizing that in some places continuous forest may exist at this elevation. Documentation of high-elevation species is ongoing; numerous taxa are probably not represented on this list, especially at the lower limits near 9,000 feet where, for example, such species as *Festuca idahoensis*, *Elymus spicatus*, *Vaccinium cespitosum*, and *Arnica latifolia* are probably present above 9,000 feet. This list is provisional and subject to change; directed collection should improve this list in the future.

ADIANTACEAE
> *Pellaea breweri* D.C. Eaton

ASPLENIACEAE
> *Athyrium alpestre* (Hoppe) Clairville var. *americanum* Butters
> *Cystopteris fragilis* (L.) Bernh
> *Dryopteris filix-mas* (L.) Schott

ADOXACEAE
> *Sambucus racemosa* L. var. *melanocarpa* (Gray) McMinn

APIACEAE
> *Angelica roseana* Henderson
> *Bupleuron americanum* Coult. & Rose
> *Ligusticum filicinum* Wats.
> *Lomatium cous* (Wats.) Coult. & Rose
> *Lomatium dissetum* (Nutt.) Math. & Const.var. *multifidum* (Nutt.) Math. & Const.
> *Lomatium triternatum* (Pursh) Coult. & Rose var. *platycarpum* (Torrey) Boivin

ASTERACEAE
> *Achillea millefolium* L. var. *lanulosa* (Nutt.) Piper
> *Agoseris glauca* (Pursh) Raf. var. *dasycephala* (T. & G.) Jeps.
> *Agoseris glauca* (Pursh) Raf. var. *laciniata* (Eaton) Smiley
> *Agoseris lackschewitzii* Henderson & Moseley
> *Antennaria aromatica* Evert
> *Antennaria corymbosa* E. Nels.
> *Antennaria flagellaris* (Gray) Gray
> *Antennaria lanata* (Hook.) Greene
> *Antennaria media* Greene
> *Antennaria microphylla* Rydb.
> *Antennaria monocephala* DC.
> *Antennaria umbrinella* Rydb.
> *Arnica longifolia* Eaton
> *Arnica mollis* Hook.

*Arnica rydbergii* Greene
*Artemisia frigida* Willd.
*Artemisia ludoviciana* Nutt.var. *latiloba* Nutt.
*Artemisa michauxiana* Bess.
*Artemisia scopulorum* Gray
*Chaenactis alpina* (Gray) Jones
*Cirsium eatonii* (Gray) Robins.
*Crepis modocensis* Greene var. *modocensis*
*Ericameria suffruticosa* (Nutt.) Nesom
*Erigeron acris* L. var. *kamtschaticus* (DC.) Herder
*Erigeron compositus* Pursh
*Erigeron formosissimus* Greene
*Erigeron lonchophyllus* Hook.
*Erigeron ochroleucus* Nutt. var. *scribneri* (Canby ex Rydb.) Cronq.
*Erigeron peregrinus* (Banks ex Pursh) Greene var. *scaposus* (T. & G. ) Cronq.
*Erigeron radicatus* Hook.
*Erigeron rydbergii* Cronq.
*Erigeron simplex* Greene
*Erigeron ursinus* Eaton
*Hieracium triste* Willd. ex Spreng. var. *gracile (*Hook.) Gray
*Hulsea algida* Gray
*Oreostemma alpigenum* (T. & G.) Greene var. *haydenii* (Porter) Nesom
*Packera cana* (hook.) Weber & Löve
*Packera dimorphophyla* (Greene) Weber & Löve
       var. *paysonii* (Barkley) Trock & Barkley
*Packera subnuda* (DC.) Trock & Barkley
*Packera werneriifolia* (Gray) Weber & Löve var. *alpina* (Gray) Dorn
*Senecio integerrimus* Nutt. var. *exaltatus* (Nutt.) Cronq.
*Senecio fremontii* T. & J.
*Senecio lugens* Richardson:
*Solidago multiradiata* Ait. var. *scopulorum* Gray
*Stenotus acaulis* (Nutt.)Nutt.
*Symphyotrichum foliaceum* (Lindl. ex DC.) Nesom var. *apricum* (Gray) Nesom
*Taraxacum ceratophorum* (Ledeb.) DC.:
*Taraxacum scopulorum* (Gray) Weber
*Tephroseris lindstroemii* (Ostenf.) Löve & Löve
*Tonestus lyallii* (Gray) A. Nels.
*Townsendia alpigena* Piper
*Townsendia condensata* Parry ex Gray var. *condensata*
*Townsendia parryi* Eaton
*Townsendia spathulata* Nutt.

## BORAGINACEAE

*Eritrichium nanum* (Vill.) Schrad.ex Gaudin var. *elongatum* (Rydb.) Cronq.
*Mertensia alpina* (Torrey) G. Don
*Mertensia ciliata* (James ex Torrey) G. Don var. *ciliata*

*Mertensia viridis* (A. Nels.) A. Nels.
*Myosotis alpestris* Schmidt

BRASSICACEAE
*Boechera angustifolium* (Nutt.) Dorn
*Boechera holboelii* (Hornem) Love & Love var. *retrofracta* (Graham) Rydb.
*Boechera lemmonii* (Wats.) Weber var. *drepanoloba* (Greene) Rollins
*Boechera lemmonii* (Wats.) Weber var. *lemmonii*
*Boechera lyallii* (Wats.) Dorn
*Boechera microphylla* (Nutt.) Dorn var. *microphylla*
*Boechera nuttallii* (Robins.) Dorn
*Boechera sparsiflora* (Nutt.) Dorn var. *sparsiflora*
*Descurainia incana* (Bernh. ex Fisch. & Meyer) Dorn var. *incana*
*Descurainia incana* (Bernh. ex Fisch. & Meyer) Dorn var. *macrosperma* (Schulz) Dorn
*Draba cana* Rydb.
*Draba crassa* Rydb.
*Draba crassifolia* Rydb.
*Draba densifolia* Nutt.
*Draba fladnizensis* Wulfen var. *pattersonii* (O. W. Schulz) Rollins
*Draba globosa* Payson
*Draba incerta* Payson var *incerta*
*Draba lonchocarpa* Rydb. var. *lonchocarpa*
*Draba oligosperma* Hook.
*Draba paysonii* Macbr. var. *paysonii*
*Draba paysonii* Macbr. var. *treleasii* (Schulz) Hitchc.
*Draba porsildii* Mulligan
*Physaria didymocarpa* (Hook.) Gray var. *didymocarpa*
*Physaria integrifolia* (Rollins) Lichvar
*Smelowskia calycina* (Steph. ex Willd.) Meyer
        var. *americana* (Regel & Herder Drury & Rollins

CARYOPHYLLACEAE
*Cerastium arvense* L. ssp. *strictum* Gaudin
*Cerastium beeringianum* Cham. & Schlecht var. *capillare* Fern. & Wieg.
*Eremogone congesta* (Nutt.) Ikonnikov var. *congesta*
*Eremogone congesta* (Nutt.) Ikonnikov var. *lithophila* (Rydb.) Maguire
*Minuartia austromontana* Wolf & Packer
*Minuartia nuttallii* (Pax) Briq. var. *nuttallii*
*Minuartia obtusiloba* (Rydb.) House
*Minuartia rubella* (Wahl.) Hiern
*Sagina saginoides* (L.) Karsten
*Silene acaulis* (L.) Jacq.
*Silene parryi* (Wats.) Hitchc. & Maguire
*Stellaria longipes* Goldie var. *longipes*
*Stellaria umbellata* Turcz.

CRASSULACEAE

    *Sedum lanceolatum* Torrey
    *Sedum integrifolium* (Raf.) A. Nels.

CYPERACEAE

    *Carex albonigra* Mack.
    *Carex aquatilis* Wahlenb. var. *aquatilis*
    *Carex capitata* L.
    *Carex duriuscula* C. A. Meyer
    *Carex elynoides* Holm
    *Carex epapillosa* Mack.
    *Carex haydeniana* Olney
    *Carex illota* Bailey
    *Carex micropoda* C.A. Meyer
    *Carex neurophora* Mack.
    *Carex nigricans* C. A. Meyer
    *Carex obtusata* Lilj.
    *Carex paysonis* Clokey
    *Carex pelocarpa* F. J. Hermann
    *Carex phaeocephala* Piper
    *Carex praeceptorum* Mack.
    *Carex raynoldsii* Dewey
    *Carex rossii* Boott
    *Carex rupestris* Allioni
    *Carex scirpoidea* Michx. var. *pseudoscirpoidea* (Rydb.) Dunlop
    *Carex scopulorum* Holm
    *Carex stenoptila* F. J. Hermann
    *Carex subnigricans* Stacey
    *Carex tahoensis* Smiley

ERICACEAE

    *Arctostaphylos uva-ursi* (L.) Spreng.
    *Phyllodoce empetriformis* (Sw.) D. Don
    *Phyllodoce glandulifera* (Hook.) Cov.

FABACEAE

    *Astragalus alpinus* L.
    *Astragalus australis* (L.) Lam var. *glabriusculus* (Hook.) Isely
    *Astragalus kentrophyta* Gray var. *tegetarius* (Wats.) Dorn
    *Astragalus miser* Dougl. var. *hylophilus* (Rydb.) Barneby
    *Hedysarum alpinum* L. var. *americanum* Michx.
    *Hedysarum sulphurescens* Rydb.
    *Lupinus argenteus* Pursh var. *depressus* (Rydb.) C. L. Hitchc.
    *Oxytropis borealis* DC. var. *viscida* (Nutt.) Welsh
    *Oxytropis campestris* (L.) DC. var. *cusickii* (Greenm.) Barneby
    *Oxytropis deflexa* (Pallas) DC. var. *foliolosa* (Hook.) Barneby

*Oxytropis lagopus* Nutt. var. *lagopus*
*Oxytropis parryi* Gray
*Oxytropis sericea* Nutt. var. *speciosa* (T. & G.) Welsh
*Trifolium haydenii* Porter
*Trifolium parryi* Gray var. *montanense* (Rydb.) Welsh

## GENTIANACEAE
*Frasera speciosa* Dougl ex Griseb.
*Gentianella tenella* (Rottb.) Boerner

## GROSSULARIACEAE
*Ribes montigenum* McClatchie

## HYDROPHYLLACEAE
*Hydrophyllum capitatum* Dougl. ex Benth. var. *capitatum*
*Phacelia hastata* Dougl. ex Lahm. var. *hastata*
*Phacelia sericea* (Grah. ex Hook.) Gray var. *sericea*

## ISOETACEAE
*Isoetes bolanderi* Engelm.

## JUNCACEAE
*Juncus drummondii* Meyer
*Juncus mertensianus* Bong.
*Juncus parryi* Engelm.
*Luzula piperi* (Coville) Jones
*Luzula spicata* (L.) DC.

## LILIACEAE
*Lloydia serotina* (L.) Salisbury ex Reichenback var. *serotina*
*Zygadenus elegans* Pursh

## LINACEAE
*Linum lewisii* Pursh var. *lewisii*

## ONAGRACEAE
*Epilobium ciliatum* Raf. var. *glandulosum* (Lehm.) Dorn
*Epilobium clavatum* Trel.
*Epilobium halleanum* Hausskn.
*Epilobium saximontanum* Hausskn.

## OPHIOGLOSSACEAE
*Botrychium* sp.

## OROBANCHACEAE
*Orobanche uniflora* L. var. *occidentalis* (Greene) Taylor & MacBryde

## PARNASSIACEAE

*Parnassia fimbriata* Konig

*Parnassia kotzebuei* Cham. ex Spreng.

## PINACEAE

*Abies bifolia* A. Murray

*Picea engelmannii* Parry ex Engelm. var. *engelmannii*

*Pinus albicaulis* Engelm.

## PLANTAGINACEAE

*Plantago tweedyi* Gray

## POACEAE

*Achnatherum nelsonii* (Scribn.) Barkw. ssp. *dorei* (Barkw. & Maze) Barkw.

*Achnatherum pinetorum* (Jones) Barkw.

*Agrostis mertensii* Trin.

*Agrostis variabilis* Rydb.

*Calamagrostis purpurescens* R. Br.

*Deschampsia cespitosa* (L.) Beauv. var. *cespitosa*

*Elymus scribneri* (Vasey) Jones

*Festuca baffinensis* Polunin

*Festuca brachyphylla* Schultes & Schultes var. *brachyphylla*

*Festuca brachyphylla* Schultes & Schultes var. *coloradensis* (Fredericksen) Dorn

*Festuca minutiflora* Rydb.

*Festuca saximontana* Rydb.

*Leucopoa kingii* (Wats.) W. A. Weber

*Melica bulbosa* Geyer ex Porter & Coult.

*Melica spectabilis* Scribn.

*Phleum alpinum* L.

*Poa alpina* L.

*Poa arctica* R. Br. var. *grayana* (Vasey) Dorn

*Poa cusickii* Vasey var. *epilis* (Scribn.) C. L. Hitchc.

*Poa fendleriana* (Steud.) Vasey ssp. *fendleriana*

*Poa interior* Rydb.

*Poa pratensis* L.

*Poa reflexa* Vasey & Scribn. ex Vasey

*Poa rupicola* Nash ex Rydb.

*Poa secunda* Presl ssp. *secunda*

*Podagrostis humilis* (Vasey) Björkman

*Trisetum spicatum* (L.) Richt.

*Trisetum wolfii* Vasey

## POLEMONIACEAE

*Phlox multiflora* A. Nels.

*Phlox pulvinata* (Wherry) Cronq.

*Polemonium* pulcherrimum Hook. var. *pulcherrimum*

*Polemonium viscosum* Nutt.

POLYGONACEAE
   *Bistorta bistortoides* (Pursh) Small
   *Bistorta vivipara* (L.) Delarbre
   *Eriogonum ovalifolium* Nutt. var. *purpureum* (Nutt.) Durand
   *Eriogonum umbellatum* Torr. var. *umbellatum*
   *Oxyria digyna* (L.) Hill
   *Polygonum austinae* Greene

PORTULACACEAE
   *Claytonia lanceolata* Pursh
   *Claytonia megarrhiza* (A.Gray) Parry ex S.Watson
   *Lewisia pygmaea* (Gray) Robins.

PRIMULACEAE
   *Androsace septentrionalis* L. var. *subulifera* Gray
   *Dodecatheon pulchellum* (Raf.) Merr. var. pulchellum
   *Douglasia montana* Gray

RANUNCULACEAE
   *Anemone multifida* Poiret
   *Anemone parviflora* Michx.
   *Anemone tetonensis* Porter ex Britton
   *Caltha leptosepala* DC.
   *Ranunculus eschscholtzii* Schlecht.var. *eschscholtzii*
   *Ranunculus eschscholtzii* Schlecht.var. *eximius* (Greene) Benson
   *Ranunculus eschscholtzii* Schlecht.var. *trisectus* (Eastw.) Benson
   *Ranunculus pygmaeus* Wahlenb.
   *Trollius albiflorus* (Gray) Rydb.

ROSACEAE
   *Dryas octopetala* L. var. *hookeriana* (Juz.) Breit.
   *Geum rossii* (R. Br.) Ser. var. *turbinatum* (Rydb.) Hitchc.
   *Geum triflorum* Pursh var. *ciliatum* (Pursh) Fassett
   *Ivesia gordonii* (Hook.) T. & G.
   *Potentilla diversifolia* Lehm. var. *diversifolia*
   *Potentilla diversifolia* Lehm. var. *perdissecta* (Rydb.) Hitchc.
   *Potentilla glandulosa* Lindl. var. *pseudorupestris* (Rydb.) Breit.
   *Potentilla gracilis* Dougl. ex Hook. var. *fastigiata* (Nutt.) Wats.
   *Potentilla gracilis* Dougl. ex Hook var. *pulcherrima* (Lehm.) Fern.
   *Potentilla nivea* L.
   *Potentilla ovina* Macoun var. *ovina*
   *Potentilla rubricaulis* Lehm.
   *Sibbaldia procumbens* L.

## RUBIACEAE
*Galium bifolium* Wats.

## SALICACEAE
*Salix arctica* Pallas var. *petraea* (Anderss.) Bebb
*Salix glauca* L. var. *villosa* (Hook.) Anderss.
*Salix reticulata* L. var. *nivalis* (Hook.) Anderss.
*Salix rotundifolia* Trautv. var. *dodgeana* (Rydb.) E. Murray

## SAXIFRAGACEAE
*Heuchera parvifolia* Nutt. ex T. & G.
*Lithophragma glabrum* Nutt. var. *ramulosum* (Suksd.) Boivin
*Mitella pentandra* Hook.
*Saxifraga adscendens* L. var. *oregonensis* (Raf.) Breit.
*Saifraga bronchialis* L. var. *austromontana* (Wieg.) Piper ex G. N. Jones
*Saxifraga cernua* L.
*Saxifraga cespitosa* L. var. *minima* Blank.
*Saxifraga flagellaris* Willd. ex Sternb. var. *crandalii* (Gand.) Dorn
*Saxifraga occidentalis* Wats.
*Saxifraga odontoloma* Piper
*Saxifraga oppo*sitifolia L.
*Saxifraga rhomboidea* Greene
*Saxifraga rivularis* L.
*Saxifraga subpetala* E. Nels.
*Telesonix heucheriiformis* (Rydb.) Rydb.

## SELAGINELLACEAE  \
*Selaginella densa* Rydb. var. *densa*
*Selaginella densa* Rydb. var. *scopulorum* (Maxon) R. M. Tryon

## SCROPHULARIACEAE
*Besseya wyomingensis* (A. Nels.) Rydb.
*Castilleja crista-galli* Rydb.
*Castilleja pallescens* (Gray) Greene
*Castilleja pulchella* Rydb.
*Castilleja rhexifolia* Rydb.
*Castilleja sulphurea* Rydb.
*Collinsia parviflora* Lindl.
*Pedicularis bracteosa* Benth. var. *paysoniana* (pennell) Cronq.
*Pedicularis contorta* Benth. var. *contorta*
*Pedicularis groenlandica* Retz.
*Pedicularis parryi* Gray var. *purpurea* C. Parry
*Penstemon attenuatus* Dougl. ex Lindl. var. *pseudoprocerus* (Rydb.) Cronq.
*Penstemon montanus* Greene var. *montanus*
*Penstemon procerus* Dougl. ex Grah. var. *procerus*
*Penstemon* whippleanus Gray

*Veronica wormskjoldii* R. & S.

## VALERIANACEAE
*Valeriana acutiloba* Rydb. var. *pubicarpa* (Rydb.) Cronq.

## VIOLACEAE
*Viola adunca* Smith
*Viola praemosa* Dougl. ex Lindl. var. *altior* Blank.

NPS 101/118316, December 2012

www.ingramcontent.com/pod-product-compliance
Lightning Source LLC
Chambersburg PA
CBHW080918290526
45795CB00007BA/2567